ODESSA

ALSO BY PATRICIA KIRKPATRICK

Century's Road

ODESSA

POEMS

PATRICIA KIRKPATRICK

 milkweed
editions

5/13

Published 2012 by Milkweed Editions
Printed in Canada
Cover and interior design by Gretchen Achilles/Wavetrap Design
Cover art by Joey Kirkpatrick, "Spooled Torso," 1998, monoprint.
Author photo by Katharine Klein Sawyer
The text of this book is set in Minion.
12 13 14 15 16   5 4 3 2 1
First Edition

Please turn to the back of this book for a list of the sustaining funders of Milkweed Editions.

Library of Congress Cataloging-in-Publication Data

Kirkpatrick, Patricia.
  Odessa : poems / Patricia Kirkpatrick. -- 1st ed.
     p. cm.
  ISBN 978-1-57131-456-7 (pbk. : acid-free paper)
  I. Title.
  PS3561.I7135O34 2012
  811'.54--dc23
                                              2012028096

This book is printed on acid-free paper.

TO SIMONE AND ANTON

and

THE MAD SISTERS

CONTENTS

This is the light of autumn, not the light of spring.
The light of autumn: *you will not be spared.*

The songs have changed; the unspeakable
has entered them. . . .

The songs have changed, but really they are still quite beautiful.
They have been concentrated in a smaller space, the space of the mind.

— LOUISE GLUCK, Averno

AURA

The vanishing road and the window lit for a second and then dark.
And then the sudden dancing light, that was hung in the future.

— VIRGINIA WOOLF

NEAR ODESSA

Near the end of summer.
Wheatfield with lark. With swift,
longspur, and sparrow. I see the birds
opening tails and wings
above grasses
and hidden nests.
Soybeans with bells, yellowing, green
tassels of corn, geese
again and again.
I see the birds
but wind takes all the sound.
Small towns are reduced to chains or storefronts,
boarded-up.
Almost to the river called a lake, gray stones of water,
dammed, white-capped, hinge
between states.
Some fields are so gold they seem to be singing.
The gold fields lie down, flat but not empty,
and will be harvested later with blades.
Near Odessa
I come to a place where the end is beginning.
Where the light is absolute, it rises.

ODESSA
for JS

I drove through Sacred Heart and Montevideo,
over the Chippewa River, all the way to Madison.
When I stopped, walked into grass —
bluestem, wild rose, a monarch —
I was afraid at first. Birds I couldn't identify
might have been bobolinks,
non-breeding plumage.
I am always afraid of what might show up, suddenly.
What might hide.
At dusk I saw the start of low plateaus, plains
really, even when planted. Almost to the Dakota border
I was struck by the isolation and abiding loneliness
yet somehow thrilled. Alone. Hardly another car on the road
and in town, just a few teenagers
wearing high school sweatshirts, walking and laughing, on the edge
of a world they don't know.
Darkness started as heaviness in the colors
of fields, a tractor, cornstalks, stone.
I turned back just before the Prairie Wildlife Refuge
at Odessa, the place I came to see. Closed.
Empty. The moon rose. Full.
I was driving Highway 7, the "Sioux Trail."
I could feel the past the way I could in Mexico,
Mayan tombs in the jungle at Palenque,
men tearing papers from our hands.
Three hours still to drive home.

BEFORE THE RED RIVER

after Journal of a Prairie Year *by Paul Gruchow (1947–2004)*

The day starts wild and sure, abundant sun
strikes fields, the ordered corn
runs in pleasured rows.

Leaves blow across the road.

But in the west a clustered storm moves
closer, sending snow across the windshield.

Sun disappears. Soon plainly visible things —
cows, the map, fences, geese, a shed —
seem left behind.

It isn't hard to picture
other people here
nor fire nor herds nor origins of weather that begin
as current meeting change.
But where is what they made?

Before the Red River flows north,
before houses with plastic
sacks of trash and oil drums
to burn garbage,

before iron wheels sparked grass along tracks
and kept going,

before cordgrass, pheasant, pasque flower,
before hides stitched by hand with sinew,
before scaffolds held bones to the wind,

ice pulled its black edge
over these basins
and left the deep earth its measure.

LETTER FROM UNITED

Of course I heard voices in the night,
saw visions,
felt the presence of dying,
that white, fringed place.
Shallow breath, narrow entrance —
the door to death opened.
Then came steroids
and lack of inhibition.
There was terror. I admit it.

Just before I learned the news
I realized all you have meant to me
and I thought I had too much feeling
to continue to spend time with you.
I had a brain tumor
and it had to come out. Damage.
Seizure and aura, the gray dome of the growth
or a cathedral lit at the top where the cross is. Flora wrote,
So much of life we find in the funniest places.

Boundaries. Love.
Bone, cutting, and stitches.
More blood than the surgeon had ever ordered.
I knew I needed your help
for the children, the family I might have to leave.

I am writing to say I can make the changes.
I am writing to say I have been opened and closed.
I am writing to say that today when the nurse came
to change my dressing,

she glanced up and said, "Oh, look, is that snow?"
We looked out the window and saw it together,
first flakes,
those white, fringed birds
flying,
the first snow of the new season.

Often they felt cold yet knew days of blistering heat. One was born after the war, then another, another, another, all wrapped, cocoon-like, in cloth. Nobody knew the time. Animals darted in grass. Spotted birds scattered like knives.

Core they call the first to go into a field the mother makes. She has a shell for an ear and hears voices, names flowers. Another keeps tools, small needles and beads, in boxes. A door in her mind leads to sky. One runs like a storm, her hair jagged current. She can't touch the vessels she makes. Another plants seeds and they grow. She keeps a fire and her table as a place for others.

In the milk stage they all harvest maize. Clean corn while the kernels are sweet. With one hand, grip the ear, silks between fingers, while the second hand pulls down the husk: let your first hand turn the ear until all the pale kernels show. Now fit the second hand around the husk. Grasping there, snap, breaking off the hidden stalk.

During that time they took everything we made. When we asked where something was they said it had broken in transport. The river was swollen and the coast putrid with sludge, but we knew nothing of that.

Music swayed in trees, the invisible weight of one leaf touching another. Gold, roan, and green. Years have gone by. The blanket shows three figures standing in a row but in life no one can count them all.

THE ABUSER: *from* THE ITALO POEMS

I was not beaten as a child
but I was in the room my sister was
and tried to pull our father off
her single thrashing body
to call for help the summer's
open window told
the neighbors and the hammered day
made sequins of the screen
the screams I couldn't stop my father's
hand her legs the welts and all her sobbing

I was not beaten as a child
but my mother's nose was broken
the war was on her mother drove them
to the hospital knowing that her father
did it is a story tunneled through
a culvert of the camp some sixty years
my mother tells me with her hands
of rationed gas and sugar you have to stop
telling bad times just remember good
I answer *no* I answer I will never

I was not beaten as a child
but I was beaten down called *stupid*
clumsy smart for talking back — for saying
what I wanted I was shown
pornography French-kissed by my
accuser locked inside the room and later

when a woman called I have hung up
ignored her given goodness rage and
mercy all the days of my life surely now
the names will follow *yes* I promise I will tell

TWO ARROWS

for Virginia Jenni Kirkpatrick (1929–2005)

The girl putting her doll to bed
in the beloved pink bassinet.

The grandmother seizing her hand at the inquest,
breaking skin.

The husband bringing lilies to the room
as a nurse wheels in their newborn.

The woman, the last day, asking at dusk,
"Is this dying?"

You return to your mother's house,
find keys, clean closets,
call an attorney.

Select music. Bach: "Sheep
May Safely Graze."
Like pacing a field to look for afterbirth.

The attorney writes back,
*The pleadings, the correspondence,
the financial documents. Toss the rest.*

Behind the house in a tree, feathers
aren't really blue on the indigo bunting

but black. Soon even with socks on your hands
you're too cold to walk any more outcrops.

A single blue heron flies low
across cordgrass, one direction,

and then another.

THE HUSBAND: *from* THE ITALO POEMS

You are a stranger. A stranger I chose
to marry.

A man I have slept beside
nine thousand sixty-three nights.

A colleague, who came in the room,
attracting me

to your face and your noble
forehead, your father's
gold Bulova, ticking, on your wrist.
Your wit, I admit, more than manners.

All that dark hair. I ran my hand
under your shirt.
Blindfolded, I'd know
the smell of you anywhere.

I delivered a daughter.
I delivered a son.
You set them in my arms
and called them ours.

Then we cooked dinner.
Bathed and read to the children.

When you sleep, a rabbit cleaves to your shoulder.
I know your dreams
as well as your habits,
the boat your mother floated
in the sink to surprise you on birthdays.

I fold colored shorts
and socks into stacks,
open the window
after you use the bathroom.

Mediocre cook that I am, I wanted
to be your hosannah.
Tonight snapper stuffed with pistachios,
another night hamburger.

All those nights I lit candles
to make the light of this house
home when you got here.

Where do you go when you're gone?

At night you bring a glass of water
to sip, then set under our bed.
I want to bring the water for you,
my stranger.

WHITE TREES

Hope is an 'intuition of emptiness' with which we make an agreement . . .

— FANNY HOWE

She went out to see
white trees
that night as black
branches turned
and filled with snow
shrouds where
lamplight
didn't reach
where figures
she went out to stay
away from
how the night went on
without her
burrow into drifts
to stalk
the blizzard to its face
and deep crevasse
to fall
and falling
to touch
silence
with her hands
to channel
vision against the coming
storm the sheen
of sodden places
as if to pick up
afterbirth

and steady lambs
to grass to
track
and shepherd
grief she walked
that night
to vacancies
white trees were filling with

THE PATIENT

In the middle of the night
I wake to a bowl on the bed
and plastic taped to my arms.
A Filipina woman is standing at my side
with two white cloths in her hands.
"Do you want to or should I?"
At first I don't know what she is asking me.
Then I do.
"I will." I lift myself
over the bowl and pull away the gown
from the place I see they have shaved.
I am not young and I am not beautiful now.
I urinate into the bowl
then take the cloths
she has been holding.
I wipe between my legs again and again
then hand back the cloths
she puts in the bowl and takes away.
I am still a woman in a body
that can be cherished, touched, or broken
like a piece of bread.
Then I lie down and cover myself.

PARIETAL

Have I made an error?

What are you saying to me & am I in-my-senses?

I didn't know where I was going.

— OJIBWE

PERSEPHONE'S ENTRY

This is a place where snow burns your feet.
The beloved disappear.

Dark always.
Some branches, loose veils, the sound
of water dripping
although the ground is saturated with ashes.

They bring food and a pail of water.
Bring fruit the color of bloodstain.

What they said to be afraid of:
Green apples. Matches.
Swimming too soon after lunch.
Talking to strangers. Not this

same day endlessly passing. Wake.
Work. Sleep alone
or crammed against others.

He wants little from me really.

Walking the corridor
I go over and over in my mind. What I did.
What I could have done
differently. What I
didn't do.

Men come at dawn and start digging.
I expect it will take a long time
to learn they find nothing.

Stolen, shut in, hidden.
Small room. Shrouds. Eye to eye
with a beak
and talons. Kept
in a low place.

Remember you are not yourself.
That's what they say when
caught off guard.
Or to protect their own interests.

Core means the innermost part.
I remember lessons
with flowers on the table, learning
the name for *papery carpels*

in the ripened ovary.
In a pome.
An apple. I remember seeing

fire on the mountain.
We held out apples to horses.

Your husband is leaving.
You have to choose.
You have to get an attorney.
Go downtown near the steeple and derelict pigeons
where the bells alone cost millions.
Walk into corporate heights, crying,
state your name at the desk,
weep at a table longer than your dining room,
decide what to keep and give up.
Smart and tough
without love, the attorney
knows the law, knows the patterns,
as birds this time of year, sensing winter and frantic
to get what they're after,
sometimes tear wings when they come to the window.
Broken, a window screen cuts but it keeps birds outside;
stays invisible enough to show light.
This is called cutting your losses.
This is called seeing the big picture. Even a kind man
speaks in numbers, measures
what was promised,
what was denied, broken, lost.
The attorney asks and your answer
costs ten thousand dollars.
You thought there was a story that made your life a river,
a corner at Clement Street and the Park Presidio Bakery
where you gave a man your dream and your man, your man
is gone now. *The train has left*
the station. No use. Listening.
Tired footsteps. Stairs.

The birds outside bathe in dust. Listen for the falcon.
Ahead of you your husband is waiting with a lover.
The attorney knows *hell hath no fury*
like you. Like yours.
No laws providing maintenance
when the roof leaks, the car floods,
you have no one to touch you and almost no
savings. The attorney draws up papers
that describe your role as parent, decide
whether to return the minor child
before or after fireworks.

You remember how you nursed the children,
how your nipples, swollen with infection, bled.
How you loved. Your husband.
This is called giving over to emotion.
This is called a business negotiation.
You've never read a spreadsheet and so must trust
the attorney to know
which judge, which statute, which waiver,
which gabardine suit to lean forward in, murmuring
"mental health issues."
The attorney represents you
but measures two sides of the story.
What is truer than the truth?
Floating rate. Income stream.
Once you touched a baby's fontanel.
The name for what the attorney touches
is money. You need an attorney
to touch money for you.

You want to keep your house and your children's
affection when you have been stupid,
torn, and forsaken.
You want to smear your hands across
the attorney's suit when you proofread the settlement.
You look out the skyscraper window
without screens, without
pigeons bobbing on ledges.
Cling to your story
and try to tell
the truth. You owe the attorney money
and you have to choose.

FAMILY COURT

To get here we carried flowers,
touched skin,
took a vow, made a child,
broke a promise.
Maybe we made mistakes.
Now change fractures the core
of lives we knew,
brings us to benches, hard seats
along the wall.

When two plates of earth
rub against each other,
having nowhere else to go,
they crack or shatter.
"Brittle failure" geologists call it.

How could it happen to us?
Bodies are mostly water.
We think people want to be good.

Outside, day lilies bloom in planters.
Inside we're screened for weapons.

We stare at hands or look across the room
where others wait too, stunned
by the passage we've booked,
the ticket that delivers us
to steerage,
the lowest deck on a journey.

Some of us are taken to small rooms.
We might have attorneys or
orders for protection,
push strollers, hide bruises with scarves.
Blinking tears we notice the man
at the door wears a gun in his holster.

The judge stays invisible until the last minute
when a gavel divides voices from silence
and the order of the court.

Far away the oldest bird in the world,
black and white and listed
in field books as "common,"
wails a long call before diving
deeper. Deeper.

PERSEPHONE'S LAMENT

Nothing has changed.
My father takes a beautiful wife.
She is not my mother.
I saw my mother struggle
to make ends meet
and I suppose
to save us.
Now she is gone.
I remember how she washed our hair
with the juice
of fresh lemons.
Now it is spring.
Fields are green. We begin
to sweep and clean.
Seeds are set in earth.
Birds fly close to the house.
I see nests of sticks and mud.
The new wife
is not my complaint.
But I remember
my mother's face
and such contortion
as she pleaded.

HIDDEN FALLS

The wind had been through
the valley
leaving everything cold
and gleaming
like bells.
Overhead, cabled towers
strung current.
I was thinking of you
and what I can't change.
Some color still hung
in trees,
mahogany, yellow,
but mostly just branches and winter
coming.
In bare maples
and cottonwoods,
I saw robins, hundreds
of familiar birds
I didn't recognize
migrating in flocks.
Walking at the Mississippi,
I was a woman, a ruin
the wind had been through.
A single bird flying over the river
flashed in the sun,
a fiery color
the eagle saw too.

BRAIN TUMOR

The plastic brain is like a snowy hill in winter.

> — NORMAN DOIDGE, *The Brain That Changes Itself,*
> describing the figure used by Dr. Alvaro Pascual-Leone to
> explain how the brain changes, yet we remain ourselves

1. *A WOMAN PERPETUALLY FALLING:* SYMPTOMS,
   TESTS, DIAGNOSIS

First you stumble and then you fall
and then you limp and hide and drop foot.
And then you lie and hide and hold
a chair before you stumble and fall again.

You know the words but still
you tremble,
fall at the board, stumble at curbs.
Step out of shoes, walk into walls.
Finally a student says after class,
"There's really something wrong with you."

They look inside you
and then they come out.
Then they hook wires to your head,
take pictures, add bells,
and although you're a woman,
you feel like a child.

Machines can do this, link the brain
language of electrical current
to patterns on paper, colored scrawls
like toddler drawings
or a Jackson Pollock painting.

Beer for stimulus,
later a hair wash.
Eyes open, eyes closed —
your brain translates you
into a line on paper: red, green
blue. Mobility, expression,
balance.

First sensed, then signaled,
every reflex, feeling, action,
even *thoughts have a physical signature*
fired in the brain,
transmitted by neurons,
measured from the scalp.

What is inside shows up
and spikes the monitor.

Brain tumor.

You stumble because your brain has been pressed
for so long, its tissue is damaged,
its current volcanic.

Now you understand the numb foot,
the jumps, floaters, and tingling.
Now you are seized and perpetually falling,
That colt didn't throw me. I threw him.

Now the walls are leaking. The doctor is sorry.
The nurses are upside down.

The apples are talking to the maple trees.
The ovens are cleaning themselves.

"thoughts too have a physical signature" — NORMAN DOIDGE,
The Brain That Changes Itself

The timer begins.
Start with *nectarine, cherry, plum.*
Blackberry, rhubarb, fig.
"You did very well," the doctor says,
then tells me to roll my tongue.
"Word-finding isn't the problem.
You can't touch your finger to your chin
when I tell you to."

Tangerine, apple, peach.
My name is the same name it's been.
Then the house takes a comb and the brush
threads an octopus.
Under the park bench a volcano rises.
Stethoscope, halo, globe.
If I know how to erect a tripod
in the desert to picture the sphinx —
I'm done.

Cantaloupe, mango, pear.
I know who the president is.
But they make me shower naked
(while the OT with a clipboard watches)
and walk down the hall on a leash.
Honeydew, lemon, grape.
(If I call it a belt, we'll forget
Abu Ghraib.)

Persimmon, currant, quince.
Now I use harder words.
Execute, rosehip, plunge.
The problem is planning ahead
when they tell me to.
Apricot, guava, date.
Purposeful, prison, blink.

Pineapple, lychee, lime.
I can't touch my finger to my chin.
You can't make me.
I don't have to do what you tell me to.
Now I'm watching my mother pinch
dough into crust to make pie.
Persimmon, currant, quince.

Tangerine, apple — insist.
My name is the same name it's been.
I know who the president is.
If I call it a belt,
we'll forget. I can't
touch my finger to my chin.
No matter the plan, I miss.
I'm the one failing the test.
Blackberry, rhubarb, fig.
Nectarine, cherry, plum.

The moon moves to an edge of sky. I close my eyes
and see a globe of ripe fruit glistening
like a pastry core. Prune kolache. Meningioma.
The mass they say is growing on my brain.

If I can't sleep, I read, Emily Dickinson, *Vanity Fair . . .*
my fingers smooth the paper pages.

I had the bed beside the window so I told stories.
My sisters slept with their mouths open,
made noises like wings hitting screen.

Summer we went to the lake. Hair in our faces.
We could smell dead fish
before we could see them,
bony, shriveled. Every morning
we ran to the shore.

Winter. Infection and fever.
I kept asking for something to drink.
Not with words *soda* or *water*
but describing green glass 7-Up comes in.
Nobody knew what I meant.

Snow without footprints or tracks.
"See that?" I asked, pointing to
a place in air. Repetitive movements
that have no purpose. Nerve endings
like places where snow touches earth.
Blurring. Oily taste. Ghost words.
Drift and erasure.

I married a man with black hair.
I dreamt we poured milk in our shoes the day we got married.
We woke overlooking a market where rabbits,
roses, and onions hung in stalls.

I couldn't quite see the outline when they showed us
our first child's heartbeat. Later,
looking at a painting, I felt the baby quicken.

The tree was circled with grease rings.
Men came in trucks and cut it down.
I must have seen that as a child. Newspaper words:
cosmonaut, Soraya, thalidomide.

Something about men climbing out of a truck
to descend on a physical task is terrifying.

My mother died and then his.
I fingered a rosary while the rabbi said Kaddish.
Our children carried coffins.

The marriage ended.

I was driving,
fractured, bereft,
void of executive function.
Until the seizure took me,
gnawing with the current of a chainsaw,
how could I tell what was wrong?

4. *ALTERED SELF:* MEDICAL DIRECTIVE

*Patient is a fifty-six-year-old female taking keppra, prozac, concerta, folic
acid, omega fish oil, and vitamin D. Two live births by caesarian section.
Part-time college professor, divorced and single, with a master's degree,
uses seat belt, consumes four cups of tea daily, walks for exercise, currently
drinking four to five glasses of alcohol per week, not sexually active, with no
tobacco use, a smoke detector, and no violence in the home.*

"Have they told you you might not be able to speak?"
Walk. Lie down. Decide.

Make a will, sign directives,
name a proxy.
Put a second name on bank accounts.
Tell the neurosurgeon you want to get well.
Wake up for the children.
Heal to do your work again.

Can live in a wheelchair but have to
be able to read and write.

You can say you want to be yourself
now that you know you never knew who that was.

You let things pile up. Didn't return
calls or answer. Couldn't say what you meant,
draw a line in the sand, ask for
what you wanted.
Walk out.

You carried a weight, busted a strobe light,
hid your lamp under baskets and wept.

You lived in a cave, took a pitch in the gut,
ran after the boomerang,
never trusted a curve to come back.
You hatched a game plan with chicken wire,
balanced a halo with sticks, threw a few grains
to some pets. Lived without believing
what you felt. Didn't give up
but you fell.

Yes. And I hurt people.

Yes. You wanted
perfection. Perfection
is a way to save the best
for yourself
or get nothing.

Beauty and suffering
keep making the world.

Falling in love
lowers the threshold at which the pleasure centers will fire.

Yes. Beauty and suffering.

I love the wrong man.
Still I put my arms around him,
breasts loose
under a hospital gown.

    "falling in love . . . " — NORMAN DOIDGE, *The Brain That Changes Itself*

5. VISIONS

I want to lick him, naked, forehead to toe,
the way a doe would tongue a fawn.

To lay a blanket on the floor, folded, in front of fire
and get inside. Lie beneath him
and be entered.
Pant the pale, rasped breath of pleasure.

But you must not touch one who doesn't belong to you.

I lie in the hospital room waiting for someone
to come and feed me.
Fill me with biscuits, bad meat, and sugar.

Roop, roop, the machine drips fluid.
There's a cord to pull for light,
a button to push for water.

The TV above the bed plays *Jeopardy*
while a therapist is giving me a test.
I beg someone to stop the noise so I can hear
what she's saying
and answer. Time is running out.

I see a cave but I can't walk.

The window trembles like a tree that, startled,
suddenly jumps, turns, leaping to deeper
brush. The deer is gone

before you see it and what you thought was certain
disappears.

She keeps giving me the test.
No one knows how to turn off the television.

The tumor is the size of a baseball.
"I prefer to say *nectarine*," the neurosurgeon explains
when she shows the picture of my brain.

The tumor is the whiteness,
borders like a wicker basket,
a haul of uncontrolled cells
pressing *what one imagines is oneself.*
Because the skull is bone
it cannot expand.

Surgery is scheduled,
steroids prescribed. Agitated
hallucinations, panic attacks.
Weakness on one side of the body.
Seizures, fatigue, loss of balance.

I keep seeing a globe,
folds of labia, a vaginal opening.

Am I seeing myself
or the place I came from?

Am I dreaming, immaterial?
Am I a chamber, haunted?

Do I take up space?

There are flowers in the room layered with flight.
Small animals scamper
and every sort of bird in dry grass whirring.

Autumn. The wild swans drift at Coole
and cathedral bells ring.
Ordinary life is overrated, the poet writes to me.
(Someone brought his note to my box early morning.)
I need ordinary life now,
fluids and a bath after surgery,
apple and fig.

I give them my name.
They wrap my legs.

Let them go inside me
with their blades and their radiance
and let them come out.
I will be here.
I can't speak for anyone else.

"what one imagines . . ." — SIRI HUSTVEDT, *The Shaking Woman*

STEALTH GUIDED CRANIOTOMY FOR LEFT-PARIETAL PARASAGITTAL TUMOR: THREE DAYS AFTER SURGERY

That center in which thought and language are coupled will still be dusky.

— CHRISTA WOLF, *Accident: A Day's News*

She woke up and thought she was dreaming.

People kept touching her and checking machines.
She thought a violin was playing *Kol Nidre*.

She remembered them taking jewelry, her shoes,
checking cavities, her almost-grown children
holding bars of the gurney.

She remembered them pushing her through
doors opened to clatter and cold instruments.

She could speak and she knew words. *Craniotomy*.

They had put her to sleep, lifted skin, drilled
a pattern of burr holes, a bone flap

to open the skull. All the time she left her body
on the table. *Parietal*.

She remembered a chart of black letters. *Along the wall.*
"The tumor is pressing the lobe that responds to
sensation," the neurosurgeon told her.

Processes language. Guides the edge of the body
in space. "It has to come out."

She remembered a rise of white granite.
To pass undetected through unknown terrain.

The outcrop of dura was what they were after. *Parasagittal.*
There must have been a portal, slippery fissure

where they could poke latexed hands. Bloody. *Between two spheres.*
Invisible. Where they could see who she was.

Faces, then flowers. Shock of mottled orchids,
pitcher of sunflowers, pink bromeliad, milk-dipped leaves.

"Enjoy your morphine," the nurse said. Hawks blinked,
hooks glistened. She saw people not really there.
An owl at the threshold flying through

the-valley-of-the-shadow-now-sheep-may-safely-graze.

Alerter, inhibitory — whatever they gave her,
she took. Morphine didn't last. She got sick after Percoset.

She couldn't tell aura from touch. Grief from incision
when a charge slid down her cheek.
Her head hurt. Her strip shave burned. She slurred manic speech.
Closed with staples, she was fastened and tied
into gowns gap-toothed as plastic sacks to put apples in.

No pocket. No place to keep secret.
She had to learn to walk, use a toilet, write her name.
When she tried to stand up, her foot sloughed like a sock.

Empty. Now tested. She waited in a bunker for transport.
If she sneezed she'd explode. She'd fall out of herself
as if *the top of my head were taken off*. Oh, the top of her head . . .

The man in the berth beside her was moaning.
She wanted to say something to him but didn't know what.
She begged not to go but they pushed her
into magnetic resonance. Where they could see what was left.

Gross total with no transfusion. Complete resection.

Voices said "Mama" and spooned chips to her tongue.
She wanted to know where she'd been.

I'll learn to walk tomorrow, she promised.
She lies empty and shorn.

She wanted to know who she was.

Tonight the patient, worn as a road after storms, has left home and no longer walks by herself. Ekram, coming into the room to remove a tray, sees the patient ate nothing. *In situ*. In the original place the name Ekram means "one who kills the goat to serve when a guest comes." She left her country at night. Whether birds stay, or migrating, go, the earth's core, covered with grasses, desert, snowdrift or outcrop, remains. Wherever birds land, the terrain, marked by the journey, transforms. *In situ* the women speak in low voices.

NIGHT VISIONS

for Franz Allbert Richter

After a period of darkness,
people come at appointed hours.

Amidst scant preparations,
they check lists,
hang a bag on the crossbar.

It's easy to see furred animals;
crow feather, rags,
winter star.

Little birds, little wings, little curtain.
Weather of sinew and bone.

Trains arrive at the station.
Half-open doors let the cold in.

Wind makes the dry stalks tremble
and haunts the infested rows.

Babies tied to cradleboards or hidden
against flesh almost smother.
Little stains, little tears, little whimpers.

Little dreams, little lies, little time.

Where are the people now?

Thrown in the holds.
Tied to each other.
Driven away.
Departed with every head bowed.

CAIRN

The gift moves toward the empty place.

— LEWIS HYDE

THE RABBIT

Sometimes, walking into the kitchen
for tea or a glass of water, I forget
my mother is dead,
my husband is gone,
my children — their childhood
is over.
In the night I look out the window,
new snow falling in the yard.
Snow covers everything
but the tracks of the rabbit
suddenly show up.
Pebbled footprints go around in circles,
then back
into bramble.
What hides the grass gives away the rabbit.
Rabbit, I know where you live now.
For a moment I forget
who I am. For a moment
I look out the window as if nothing had happened.

THE AMYGDALA BLUES

The emotional core of your brain . . . allows you to gauge the emotional significance of what you are looking at.

— V. S. RAMACHANDRAN

A disconnection between the amygdala and the inferotemporal cortex . . . mock[s] any trust one put[s] in consciousness.

— RICHARD POWERS

There's a gray light and film over moments.
Gray light and veil over time.
Horses were turned loose in the child's sorrow.

There's a place in the brain that remembers.
A place in the brain that can tell.
The stall that the horse returns to.

Fragrance of wood smoke and hyssop.
Fragrance of wood smoke and hair.
Triggering cascades of fear.

There's whiplash and wingspan and shadow.
Whiplash and wingspan and drift.
Blizzard and gallop ahead.

Is it predator, accident, warning?
Predator, accident, friend?
Is it time? Are we there? Are you certain?

Not recognizing the familiar —
Not knowing what you can tell.
Reasoning gets distorted. Breakfast bursts into tears.

How will I know what your name is?
How will I find you again?
Electric sequence starts giving off charges . . .

eros and circuit and panic.
Rapture and whinny and lust.
No more excuse or explanation.

They are coming to board up the windows.
They are coming to board up the house.
There's a letter, a keyhole, a cleft.

In a small room they ask you to name it.
In a small room they ask what you did.
Rapid heart rate and stress-induced hormones.

Nothing comes in order.
Nothing comes in order but surges.
Hound dog aroused at the window.

Children sequestered and smokestacks.
Children sequestered with mothers.
They were told they were going to get showers.

When I woke up I was dreaming.
When I woke up I was dreaming.
Time gone was present again.

Slow down, it's only a story.
Slow down, it's only pretend.
Not everyone wants to hurt you.

Put your head down, it's almost over.
Put your head down and let the horse run.
There's a gray light and film over everything.

"Horses were turned loose . . ." — CAROLYN FORCHÉ, *Blue Hour*

TIME OF THE FLOWERS

VISION TEST

The brain, like the earth, lies in layers.
Floaters dart and punch. I see the field.
My face stays numb. "Keep your eye on the target.
Click the button when a light appears."
At home I read, *So little evidence is left of what
had vanished.* I can't always follow directions.
The tumor pressed a lobe, charging
the amygdala, emotional core of the self.
In school they taught us that soil covers core
and mantle; mythology explains creation
and change. Now age drapes childhood;
my hair, the incision. I see a light but forget
to click. I didn't remember dreams for a year.
How I've changed may not be apparent.

"So little evidence . . ." — LAURIE SHECK, *The Willow Grove*

SURVIVOR'S GUILT

How I've changed may not be apparent.
I limp. Read and write, make tea, boiling water
as I practiced in rehab. Sometimes, like fire,
a task overwhelms me. I cry for days, shriek
when the phone rings. Like a page pulled from flame,
I'm singed but intact: I don't burn down the house.

Later, cleared to drive, I did outpatient rehab. Others
lost legs or clutched withered minds in their hands.
A man who can't speak recognized me
and held up his finger, meaning "one year since
your surgery." Mine. Sixteen since his. Guadalupe
wishes daily *to be the one before*. Nobody
is that. Like love, the neurons can cross fire.
You don't get everything back.

TIME OF THE FLOWERS

IN EXTREMIS

You don't get everything back.
Is today morning or night? The radio voice says
the composer is changing the place home is.
When they try to put a tube down her throat,
the woman beside me sobs. Nurses probe
a vein as she thrashes, call the Hmong translator.

Once a student told me, in Laos he sat in a tree
all night. *Father pay me dollar for every man I'm shooting.*
When there's water to cross, the fish, caught,
get needled through gill slits. Down the dark hall,
machines bleat at each bed. Eyes open, shut. Flashes,
detachment, vitreous gel. Her seven-year-old son
comes after school, peels oranges, watches football,
changing the place home is.

TIME OF THE FLOWERS

FISSURE

Changing the place home is,
you had left. Taken your things. If something hidden
is pressing, then taken, what opens? The crack
from a break or parting begins in response
to stress. *Don't come back.* You made me carry
what wasn't mine. Now I'm the wife talking to
the husband, feeling anguish, anger,
rage and grief, *ancient words for strangle.*

Now I'm the woman, kneeling in grass to pull apart
a rootbound plant, tangled in terra-cotta.
Now I'm the tumor speaking to dura mater: *Easy
to press.* Am I more for what they've taken or less
for what I've lost? The vase cracked but I put in narcissus.
It was at last the time of the flowers. . . .

"*ancient words for strangle*" — PETER SACKS, *The Poet's Notebook*
"*It was at last . . .*" — PAUL GRUCHOW, *Journal of a Prairie Year*

TIME OF THE FLOWERS

PERSEPHONE

It was at last the time of the flowers. To see
the flowers and know some wildness herself,
a girl went to the edge of a field. I've done it,
gone where I was forbidden, reached to touch
power on the stem. The earth opened to black horses,
a chariot. Seized, the girl was driven by Hades to hell.

In the modern world a boy named Jacob was riding his bike
near cornfields, aster, columbine, when it happened
to him. Don't blame the victim. Zeus, her father,
gave Persephone to Hades but the sacrifice really
happened at birth. Even if the mother is a queen,
the father has authority over women and children.
I want to call Hades, brother of Zeus, what he was.
The predatory aspect of patriarchal culture.

"It was at last . . ." — PAUL GRUCHOW, *Journal of a Prairie Year*

TIME OF THE FLOWERS

A SONG APART

Ceres, goddess of corn, grieved and raged
for her stolen daughter. They say she withheld
the harvest. But corn was already here.
The first cornfield was the beginning of settled life on earth.
"Spirit grain," the Anishinaabe called it.
Then blades of a steel plow dug short cuts
to fortune. Settlers came. *Soon the plow dug*
deep into the hunting grounds, the children died,
and their fires went out from shore to shore.

Zeus let Persephone visit each year. Shared custody.
Seeing her child, Ceres returned to green fields.
The attorney wrote: *She still retains a great deal of anger.*
Tribes were driven from the river.
the sound of their weeping   comes back to us

"*The first cornfield . . .*" — EDITH HAMILTON, *Mythology*
"*Soon the plow . . .*" — MERIDEL LESUEUR, *North Star Country*
"*the sound of . . .*" — *Anishinaabe Lyric Poems,* GERALD VIZENOR, *tr.*

TIME OF THE FLOWERS

TORN ENTRY

The predatory aspect of patriarchal culture
looks normal enough. Doctor, teacher, priest.
Forceps, field trip, Roman collar.
They make you feel special. Then
they abandon you. Then . . . *invaded earth . . .*
returns in hellish chemical

and in the tiniest spring violet. After my sister was raped,
I wrote in a notebook, buried
torn pages in dirt.

The man began to do what he did to me.
I knew no one would come.
I lay still, afraid I would never wake up.
There was nothing to do but
let the voice come through me.

"invaded earth . . ." — MERIDEL LESUEUR, *North Star Country*

61

TIME OF THE FLOWERS

THE FIELDS

Let the voice come through me.
Some who've been taken don't want to talk.
They come out squinting, or disappear
forever. Persephone is near then.
If you've lived in an apartment, you know
how it sounds when someone walks overhead.

At the roof of the underworld, the self splits
where flowers *rise on stems that thrust themselves
above . . . grassland floor.* They say a victim often flies
to the ceiling. I don't think she leaves her body
so much as escapes to a place she thinks is closer
to where someone might save her. And the campion,
switchgrass: *Aren't the fields changed by what happened?*
The earth, like the brain, lies in layers.

"*rise on stems . . .*" — PAUL GRUCHOW, *Journal of a Prairie Year*
"*Aren't the fields . . . ?* " — CAROLYN FORCHÉ, *The Angel of History*

GAMMA KNIFE

I'll put my head in a metal frame
to live longer.
I'll take off my clothes,
be pushed into a chamber.
I'll pay a doctor thousands of dollars.

The tumor's recurring.
I'll get four metal screws to the skull.
Targeted beams of radiation
because brain damage
is easier to prevent than reverse.

Tonight I listen to music, alone,
although I have children
I love. I'll get letters from friends.
Maybe flowers.
I'll smell lilacs and phlox when it's over.

Neighbors come home.
I hear car doors.
Birds stir like cards being shuffled.
All my life what wasn't enough
is suddenly what I want.

The search engine says *steppes,*
a crater in Texas,
or port on the Black Sea.
But there are no samovars
in this Odessa,
little town on the Minnesota–
Dakota border
the railroad came through
to lay tracks through prairie grass,
agents of fire, and blizzards.
Now a red water tower shaped like a rocket.
Baseball diamond. Bait-
and-tackle shop.
The plaque near a cairn
says the town was named for a daughter
of the first station agent,
who died of diphtheria at age three.
No mention of Russia
or the Greek name Odysseus
which means "angry man."
No mention of a mother.
The jail, built in 1913, hardly
big enough for a horse,
remains on the National Historic Register.
No insulation
but brick walls, barred windows,

dirt floor. Damage
and grief, one stone
then another.
Dakota before European.
What they couldn't take
they left.

SEASON
after Hsiang Hung

1. WINTER VISIT

My head is white, my hair
cut short now.
When I look in the mirror
I hardly know who I am.
But that has been true for some time
even before I was sick.
I know you came to visit.
I don't remember what we said.
"Fresh flowers," you noticed
when I brought tea to the table.
I was happy the whole time you were here.
When you left,
I held the door open,
winter moon lighting snow
as you went.
Spring will come.
I don't know if you'll visit again.
On my desk for days
I've left the cup of oolong
your lips touched.

2. SPRING

When snow melts,
the river opens.
I walk there every day, certain
I will see you.
I see tulips, narcissi,
a willow standing near the water.
Birds I have never seen before.
Your name runs ahead of me
like a furrow in earth.

3. SUMMER EVENING

I waited for you in the summer evening
but you did not come.
I set my chair in the grass,
notebook and pen in my lap,
little table beside me.
You said you wanted
to talk about what I had written.
I looked for a man
to come riding with windblown hair.
Sometimes I got up
to move the hissing sprinkler
or tip the pitcher
into my glass.
Neighbors came out when red lights and a siren
stopped up the block.
Men entered the house.
No one knew what had happened.
Soon I sat alone again,
hands astray,
each blade at my feet
single and green.
You did not come.

4. AUTUMN

The first time you came to this house
I opened the door and leaves
blew in.
I remember leaves all over the floor.
We were polite
and fumbled with words.
Now leaves blow up the street
and lights shine in windows.
Small fires burn faintly
but don't go out.

THE MUSE: *from* THE ITALO POEMS

He made her know desire again.
How troublesome its coming is.
Its black waist walking — belted and untouchable —
away from her and down the hall.

Small rooms along the way.
How much we want and can't have.
How much we can.

He handed her a key she couldn't keep.
She wanted to.

She took the purple tulip bulbs
stuck in loam and terra-cotta,
put them in the coldest corner of the basement.
She waited.
Like a prairie,
two-thirds of her was living underground.
But no one knows, she told herself.

Nobody knows.
She sent them all away.
And then aroused, entitled, secret,
she challenged an intruder
to call her and claimed

the details of her longing:
his hands, his rye-colored hair
riffled when he tired,
the grief, stubborn and wild, of his brows.

With little light, with bias,
with restless cloth and lilacs
in a cup beside the bed, with desire
he made her know again.

AFTER ODESSA

Why is it delusion to regret

when everything is given
and given, never ceases

but is changed

what has been lost

the grass, pristine
water and shards

before the corn was wheat

but sanity to trust

fields burned to save
the earth I did

truly love you   my love
for you lost

in what has not yet happened

THE GIFT
for Sally Wingert

When I was heartsick, it came
via courier, a gift I didn't know
was coming and the surprise alone
made it sweet.
When it was gone, I knew it had been
exquisite, pieces set
like precious
stone from the most
beautiful country.
It came with a knock on the door and the gait
of a man who walks rising
on the balls of his feet. Its coming,
remembered, reminded me
of living.
But the gift didn't last
or take away sorrow. No,
delivered, the gift
couldn't keep me
from grief
or emptiness. I still had to do
what was asked
and after I did, I looked on the same
withered place.
But when that box came, rustling
with luscious red tissue, I took
what was given.

RABBITS

among us
their breathing
sides slim
bellows
brown loaves soft

ears
like candles
tulip
petals quick
grace in the grass

mostly alone except
when a pair
comes at dusk or dark
jiggered haunches
running after

each other like hot
lines of lead
the inked point
of bristles a brush
with death etched

in snow against pavement
hundreds of years
after Dürer after Bashō
gnawed rose
lost

violet
near the labor of birth
let its tremor begin
on a moonlit
hill to forage

crabapples
the round eye of one
rabbit
holding this flicker
of wilderness

still

THE DOOR TO EVERYTHING AND NOTHING
for Carol Bly (1930–2007)   *for Cary Eustis*

There isn't much to say about the door really.
Trees lean. Leaves fall.
Grass is still green in late November.
A fieldstone wall,
higher than a man or woman's shoulder,
straddles the hill that rises to the cathedral.
Sometimes there's sun.
Sometimes shadow.
Sometimes just gray out the hospital window.
People lie in these beds and suffer and suffer
sometimes for what looks like
no purpose. At least to me.
I am getting better. Still I think of Keats
dying alone in Rome, saying to Dr. Severn at the end,
"Don't be frightened — be firm, and thank God it has come!"
I hear nurses in the hall phone their children,
tell them to return library books,
what kind of soup they are making for dinner.
Tell another nurse to give morphine to room 411.
There isn't a door in the wall really.
The stones just stop and turn inward.
Suddenly there's a slender darkness
going inside you can enter.
It reminds me of the darkness between two lines
on language tests I've been taking, a code that means "house"
if I can remember to say it. *House.*
I keep failing the tests but writing poems anyway.
There isn't much to say about the door.

The wall stops and the stones
turn inward.
I have no idea what you find when you enter that door.
No idea what you find when you enter that darkness.
No idea at all.

In "Brain Tumor," the title *"A Woman Perpetually Falling:* Symptoms, Tests, Diagnosis," quotes from Norman Doidge in *The Brain That Changes Itself.*

"Sensory Ghosts: Patient History," comes from the term originally used by the nineteenth-century neurologist Silas Weir Mitchell to describe the sensations, often painful, experienced by patients after losing a limb. Mitchell wrote that such patients carry "a constant or inconstant phantom of the missing member, a sensory ghost . . . sometimes a most inconvenient presence, faintly felt at the time, but ready to be called up to his perception by a blow, a touch, or a change of wind," (*Injuries of Nerves and Their Consequences,* 1872). More recently, doctors have referred to this phenomenon as a "phantom limb."

"Altered Self: Medical Directive," is so titled after Antonio Damasio's dicussion of consciousness in *The Feeling of What Happens.*

"Some Kind of Force Inside Her: Prognosis," is borrowed from Yuri Danilov, as quoted by Norman Doidge in *The Brain That Changes Itself.*

"The Italo Poems" were written in response to the work of artist Italo Scanga (1932-2000).

ACKNOWLEDGMENTS

I thank the editors of the following journals in which these poems first appeared:

Agni Online: "The Fields" (from "Time of the Flowers")

Flurry: "Winter Visit," "Spring" (from "Season")

Great Twin Cities Poetry Review: "A Woman Perpetually Falling: Symptoms, Tests, Diagnosis" (from "Brain Tumor")

New South: "The Patient," "Persephone's Lament"

Poetry East: "The Rabbit," "The Gift"

Poetry: "Vision Test," "Survivor's Guilt," and "In Extremis" (from "Time of the Flowers")

Prairie Schooner: "The Abuser: *from* The Italo Poems," "Two Arrows"

Saint Paul Almanac: "Letter from United," "The Door to Everything and Nothing," and "A Song Apart" (from "Time of the Flowers")

Seminary Ridge Review: "Stealth Guided Craniotomy for Left-Parietal Parasagittal Tumor: Three Days After Surgery"

What Light: "Near Odessa," "Rabbits"

I want to thank the law firm of Lindquist & Vennum. I am honored to be the first recipient of the Lindquist & Vennum Prize for Poetry and grateful for the attention this award brings to the art of poetry, which, from ancient roots, flourishes and enriches contemporary life in the Midwest. My thanks especially to Daniel Slager and Allison Wigen at Milkweed Editions, and to Peter Campion. I thank the Loft, the McKnight Foundation, and the Minnesota State Arts Board for fellowships, which enabled me to complete the work in this book, and for supporting the work of writers and artists.

I am grateful to Dr. Jane Kilian, Dr. Mary Dunn, Dr. Diane Chappuis, Dr. William Davis, Dr. Deanna Dickens, Dr. Paul Sperduto, Christine Sheetz, Sue Newman, the staff of the Sister Kenny Rehabilitation Institute at United Hospital in Saint Paul and at Abbott Northwestern Hospital in Minneapolis, many unnamed nurses and caregivers, and especially to Karrol Butler. My thanks to Jennifer Jameson.

My deepest gratitude to Kris Kirkpatrick and Michael Levine, Joey Kirkpatrick and Flora Mace, Tracy Kirkpatrick and Catherine Ross, Tim Danz and Sally Wingert, Kathy and Chuck Sawyer, Joan Swearingen Bosque, Laura David, Sally Dixon, Nimo Farah, Kathryn Greenbank, Nor Hall, Phebe Hanson, Margaret Todd Maitland, Eleanor Lerman, Jim Moore, Kimberly Nightingale, Laura Nortwen, Joyce Sutphen, Linda Tesner, and Connie Wanek.

PATRICIA KIRKPATRICK is the author of *Century's Road* (Holy Cow! Press, 2004), as well as several chapbooks of poetry. Her work has appeared widely in journals including *Prairie Schooner, Poetry, Agni Online, Threepenny Review, Saint Paul Almanac,* and *Antioch Review,* and additionally in several anthologies, among them *Robert Bly in This World* (University of Minnesota Press, 2011) and *She Walks in Beauty: A Woman's Journey Through Poems,* edited by Caroline Kennedy (Hyperion Voice, 2011). She is the recipient of fellowships from the National Endowment for the Arts, the Bush Foundation, Minnesota State Arts Board grants, and two Loft-McKnight awards. Kirkpatrick lives in Saint Paul, Minnesota.

MILKWEED EDITIONS

Founded as a nonprofit organization in 1980, Milkweed Editions is an independent publisher. Our mission is to identify, nurture and publish transformative literature, and build an engaged community around it.

JOIN US

In addition to revenue generated by the sales of books we publish, Milkweed Editions depends on the generosity of institutions and individuals like you. In an increasingly consolidated and bottom-line-driven publishing world, your support allows us to select and publish books on the basis of their literary quality and transformative potential. Please visit our Web site (www.milkweed.org) or contact us at (800) 520-6455 to learn more.

MILKWEED EDITIONS, a nonprofit publisher, gratefully acknowledges sustaining support from Maurice and Sally Blanks; Emilie and Henry Buchwald; the Bush Foundation; the Patrick and Aimee Butler Foundation; Timothy and Tara Clark; Betsy and Edward Cussler; the Dougherty Family Foundation; Mary Lee Dayton; Julie B. DuBois; Joanne and John Gordon; Ellen Grace; William and Jeanne Grandy; Moira Grosbard; John and Andrea Gulla; Elizabeth Driscoll Hlavka and Edwin Hlavka; the Jerome Foundation; the Lerner Foundation; the Lindquist & Vennum Foundation; Sanders and Tasha Marvin; Robert E. and Vivian McDonald; the McKnight Foundation; Mid-Continent Engineering; the Minnesota State Arts Board, through an appropriation by the Minnesota State Legislature and a grant from the National Endowment for the Arts; Christine and John L. Morrison; Kelly Morrison and John Willoughby; the National Endowment for the Arts; Ann and Doug Ness; Jörg and Angie Pierach; the RBC Foundation USA; Deborah Reynolds; Cheryl Ryland; Schele and Philip Smith; the Target Foundation; and Edward and Jenny Wahl.

THE McKNIGHT FOUNDATION

BUSH FOUNDATION

MINNESOTA STATE ARTS BOARD

ART WORKS.
arts.gov

TARGET.

CLEAN WATER LAND & LEGACY AMENDMENT

jerome foundation

Interior design by Gretchen Achilles/Wavetrap Design

Typeset in Minion

by Gretchen Achilles

Printed on acid-free 100% postconsumer waste paper

by Friesens Corporation

MILKWEED EDITIONS

and

THE LINDQUIST & VENNUM FOUNDATION

are pleased to announce the first award of

THE LINDQUIST & VENNUM
PRIZE FOR POETRY

to

PATRICIA KIRKPATRICK

The annual, regional prize awards $10,000 and publication by
Milkweed Editions to a poet residing in North Dakota, South
Dakota, Minnesota, Iowa, or Wisconsin. The 2012 Lindquist &
Vennum Prize for Poetry was judged by Peter Campion,
author of *Other People* and *The Lions*.

Established in 2011, the Lindquist & Vennum Prize for Poetry
celebrates poets for their artistic contributions and brings
outstanding regional writers to a national stage. Finalists are
selected from among all entrants by the editors of
Milkweed Editions. The winning collection is selected
annually by an independent judge.

Milkweed Editions is one of the nation's leading independent
publishers, with a mission to identify, nurture and publish
transformative literature, and build an engaged community
around it. The Lindquist & Vennum Foundation was
established by the Minneapolis-headquartered law firm of
Lindquist & Vennum, PLLP, and is a donor-advised fund of
The Minneapolis Foundation.